BLOOD MACHINE

Winner of the 2025 Open Chapbook Competition

poems by

KB Kinkel

Finishing Line Press
Georgetown, Kentucky

BLOOD MACHINE

ACKNOWLEDGMENTS

Some of these poems appeared, occasionally in previous forms, in literary
magazines and journals. I am grateful to the following publications for
featuring drafts of these poems:

Ninth Letter—"Recambrian"
Poetry Online—"Well"
Prelude—"Looking at You, Body"
The Rumpus—"Transmigration"
The Paddock Review—"Loss [Ambiguous]"

Publisher: Leah Huete de Maines
Editor: Christen Kincaid
Cover Art: *Divine Consequence (Terra Reverentia Study)*, 1995, Todd Bartel
Author Photo: Dee Tran
Cover Design: Elizabeth Maines McCleavy

Order online: www.finishinglinepress.com
also available on amazon.com

Author inquiries and mail orders:
Finishing Line Press
PO Box 1626
Georgetown, Kentucky 40324
USA

Contents

I

Well.. 1

The Image 1: [Consumes the Event] 2

The Image 2: [Exalts the Event] 3

Watching the Festival 4

Loss [Ambiguous] 5

Recambrian 6

Looking at you, body 8

Light Sentence.. 10

Transmigration 11

II

You Never Die the Evening [Before Your Death]........................ 15

[sound of water falling / and cars –] 17

Paper, Recovered.. 18

I Have Promises to Keep... 19

The Physical Impossibility Of 20

Given States.. 22

Cinema.. 25

Tumbling Woman.. 26

When You Look Back Into the Years That Made Your
    Own Face.. 28

I

WELL

Your body rests at the bottom of a well. This is an image.
It is your portrait, but also a machine
made to write in your lungs the language of air.

Looking down, you see how to paint the meeting of centuries.
One year glazes into another—
the first state both forgets and carries the last.

There is a sky tunnel between memory
and the blood machine that prints its pictures.
The dark water in which your body rests

is also the screen on which you appear.
They speak here: a body's waves, its mouth returning
redacted truths.

In each stratum, the data
never not meant to be unwritten.
This is not an image.

You say I have so much to unwrite for you, body.
You say, Hold out your arms,
Look up—

THE IMAGE

1: [Consumes the Event]

It was only quarter to six on the Pacific coast
but almost no one in the world had not seen

your picture. By then, you were a jagged line
in glass and aluminum skin. Also, a long cloud.

Your mouth did not yet speak but poured language
of trades that was at least as old as the fall

of the Ottoman Empire. You knew no languages
and were quickly being translated. Somewhere

everyone learned your name. Clothed in pale
blue, you were immediate cause for concern.

For seventeen minutes you held your viewers
in un-knowing. Your single plume drifted almost

softly down the Jersey Shore. You could be in two cities
at once and also absorb sky. You could be in

every city, and were. You were intimate to each room
with a cable connection. You were fire and dust

and capital—you were phone cords and wallets
and single shoes. You were at least one child's first

guilt. You were hours or decades. You were two tours
abroad, and also blazing light in a Cuban prison

yard. You were slips of paper like aspen leaves
turning as they fell. You were

the falling. You
are the dust that settles into all things.

2: [Exalts the Event]

A plane is reaching altitude. It is one
of many planes. Somewhere below is the last
hour of a girl's youth and about time
for her to do geometry. Free-bleeding
into a chair recommended for kindergarten
to grade three, she stuffs her box-pleat skort
with Angel Soft tissue. A grownup rolls a television set
into the classroom and says something is wrong
in New York. The girl is wearing hoops
for the first time. A dust cloud emerges, many
times over. The grownup flips between two channels
but both send the same pictures. The girl's socks
have small ruffles around the top hems. Pale
blue. The dust cloud contains laborers and labor itself
and she considers labor for the first time, imagines
what it would feel like for a heart to beat in her
stomach. Each time the channel switches, the images
are the same, but also, a little different. The voices
commenting on the images also change.
This reflects time passing.

WATCHING THE FESTIVAL
After Frank Bidart

What did you see when you first woke
to your guilt?

In the ten breaths
between pavement and air

the next century's fury
has already begun to take shape.

Any carved heart can be made
to justify.

You fasten your anger
to the world's anger

so that even in the cleanest light,
you fulfill and defy your desire to be good.

Wishing to leave a trace,
you turned all ice to water.

LOSS [AMBIGUOUS]

When you call to the dead, who answers?
Do you call upon space or earth's deep places?
To the bottom of a well? Or down below the sea?
Are you still her child if she doesn't remember?
Are you still married if you never found a body?
Do you call the moment of falling 'apocalypse' or 'dust'
or 'god'? And who sits, waiting, in its empty rooms?
Do you save the voicemail?
How long will you keep waiting?
What did time say to the mall built in the shape of an eye?
Who uses the rooms at Abu Ghraib?
Or who inhabits them now?
What kind of glass would make you feel safest?
And how far from the road should we build?
What do you do with found socks and gloves?
Do you still think about them?
Why did you think everything would be easier?
Why did you go back down into the cave?
Why didn't you get onto an elevator?
Why did you let them see you that way?
Why don't you call?
Why do you keep calling?
Do you feel guilty about the prisoners held without bail?
Do you think there's anything you could do?
What happens when light hits an object?
Has anyone tried to comfort you?
Has anyone asked you to carry anything for them?
Why is the air so quiet this time of year?
Do you hear those crickets?
Why is the sky so clear after a storm?
Is my beloved in your lungs?
Is my beloved in the treads of your shoes?
How much is their life worth, in American dollars?
Where can I find you among the gray clouds?
I mean, where are you?

RECAMBRIAN

You live two decades a desert
        your seasons imperceptible.

Flamed clean, you are a moth's memory
        of air.

They give you a name, then
        that means *pure*—

in these quicklime days,
        even beloved bodies dissolve

fast as the crescent on the cottontail,
        the silence it leaves.

When the rains come, you feel them only
        as longing— aster smear

along the mountain ridge, soft beating
        on the hardpan caked. The kind of rain

that falls until even the saguaros forget
        what a century is. In time

you turn amphibious, two lives:
        will boast your ribbed belly

to a nearer moon. These shrinking lungs
        can only signify a revolving back

into water, into heat— shallow seas
        where matter only potentiates

all your possible selves.
        Wading in this rising salt

preludes impossible return
       to a previous world.

To pull your body through these currents
       you must learn not to need this air.

LOOKING AT YOU, BODY

Bound, in a glass box,
in eight feet of water,
your hair fans.
Did you forget the key
in your pocket?

*

The whale may have been—is—
a symptom of the sea you lost.
For a day, into night
without a ship
you floated on the coffin
of the body of your friend—
I conceded you above mind, then.

*

In John Singleton Copley's painting of the men in the boat
and the shark under
you're the Whistler nocturne that won't be painted for another
century
but will be better loved.

*

When a thought is set out undone
in a small boat on a green sea
and singing happens
you're a distant mountain,

waiting.

*

I don't believe in the goodness
of what moves you.

*

Take out the key. swallow it.

LIGHT SENTENCE

Mona Hatoum, 1992
36 wire mesh compartments, electric motor, light bulb

You fell too early.
Not at first shift of seasons
but in an untimely way
or in a new kind of time
without a natural name.

Like dark-spiraled snails
who draw white rivers
on low-lying leaves
you sleep during heat
hold water and wake

in hours now called 'blue.'
Things are tender
or vanished. Gray wing,
feather; a smell
(almost sweet)

of a dead bird or rabbit
in a yard. In a room
a lightbulb falls, rises.
Falls. Shadow casts cages over
a place you once slept.

TRANSMIGRATION

It's halfway through autumn
and too hot for walking.

This is not an allegory.

Each week, when rice and soaps
run low, you go out

among roaming eyes, mouthless

faces and carry back what you think
will sustain. It must all be cleaned,

which takes time. The rest is spent

waiting. Against an immeasurable real
desire, old as dust, to make something

and thus survive.

Also known: scales in your teeth
are those of your own frightened tail.

To the extent that a contract binds

this soul to this body—as light
to its linen shade—

you fear—not just a release

of terms, but complicity in binding.
Is this

guilt?

Particles mote from your aerosol
expiation.

You've done this before, you know. In so many bodies.

II

YOU NEVER DIE [THE EVENING BEFORE YOUR DEATH]

Dust silences the city.
Before that, a building falls.
Before that, another.
And before that, they stand. Papers
are filed or moved toward filing.
Before that a top-floor chef
says he's forgotten chervil.
He rides the lifts up, then down—
before that a bodega roll-up's
 chain-haul rumble. A gull passes over.

Before that two high beams strike night.
A truck on an airport road.
The driver waits—two deer, one
still speckled, make a clear crossing.
Before that a child holds a cricket
in a jar, adds sticks to make it
feel at home. A quick stall
at the metal detector.
Canning jar- tinplate lid
punched with holes.

Before that, a slow-coming storm—
office lights stay on, flicker once
on a building's upper floors.
Before that rolled white cuffs
are unrolled, loosed white ties re-tighten
talking necks. Before that an office
faces an office across. A shadow
as rain slips in. Before it is black, the scene
is blue-gray. Some blazes are ships
coming into harbor.

Before the storm, a false deep—
before the deep, a single drop
on a long pane. In the pane, a start
and end. Before the city, other cities.
Before cities meet, the fingers
 in every black-oil well. Before the well, near-silence
of an un-razed village.
Dog's scratch, boy's first courtyard steps—
the sounds of voices;
the concept of beauty
and space—over the morning landfill,
a dark kite hanging overhead.

[sound of water falling and cars—]

"it gets dark in there, sometimes"

Water will decide the names.

What has been born from sound and

Everything desires to go

absence

swamp oak, swamp oak

swamp oak, swamp oak

swamp oak, swamp oak

swamp oak, swamp oak

where names go

sound of water falling and cars

absence made of absence

absence made of absence

PAPER [RECOVERED]

H—— (a man).

Relies on cold but exceeds it.

-visit?

-contacted?

-who you spoke w/

-last spoke with

-

- [   ]   died 2 yRs ago   [DATE]

when did it start?
when did it stop?
did it stop?

I am beyond a kind of fence; brightness.

Falling, I did not know—

I HAVE PROMISES TO KEEP

Achievement, admission, ashtray.
Badge, breathing machine. Bib, burn cast.
Clave, commemorative coin, cross.
Dog tag, dress shirt, duffel bag. Dust.

Emblem. Epaulets. Evidence.
Face mask. Flag [recovered]; fragment.
Glass, gown, grappler claw, gun holster.
Handcuffs. Headset. Hockey stick. Hood.

ID, inhaler, insurance.
Jacket, jersey, jewelry, journal.
Keys [recovered]; knife [recovered].
Lace. Letters. Limestone. Lunchbox. Lure.

Nameplate; napkin; needlework. Notes.
Oil stock, ornament. Pager.
Paper money. Permit. Poem. Purse.
Quilt. Record album. Respirator.

Sandals, saw, singlet. Slurry wall.
Timeline. Tissue flowers. Tribute.
Union card; urn. Utility.
Vacuum bag, vase. Voting machine.

Wallet. Whistle. Wristwatch. Wreath.

THE PHYSICAL IMPOSSIBILITY OF

1: In a fugue on violence, ocean, and 'man,' the reader argued,
"all terrorists are amateurs." Behind him, a giant glass wall and a
giant Norway spruce, planted eighty years earlier. As he spoke,
the spruce turned burned-black outline against palest blue.
The evening was touched by swallows that looked like dark
semicolons.

2: The poem was organized around the recurring and ominous
dorsal fin of a great-white shark. Something about the speaker's
terror at the sea's insatiable maw. A terror spliced with the
terrorism of being a fisherman. The moment of that terror's
transition.

3: His audience grew closer, masked and warm. It was an orange
wood hall at an elite prep school. They experienced collective
surprise at this pronouncement of this subspecies of fear. They
entered a place where images are paper in water. And the body is
paper in a solution of water and bleach.

4: "For the love of" is the root of one. It is the root of, "who
does something not professionally, but for the love of it." "Inept,
incompetent, unpaid." Etymology sets a steel metric in water.
To know expertise but not make its sounds through infinitely
replaceable teeth, or say its name in any language.

5: This one was a tiger, though the white is often substituted. Any
sex will do. What is required is a body capable of most muscular
streaming. To honor the capture and killing of the largest possible
specimen, suspension was suggested. In formaldehyde and bleach
in a long glass vitrine. It was made specifically for that purpose.

6: If the original begins to deteriorate, the original can be infinitely replaced. Replacement does not require specificity, but belief in the infinite. Like an open mouth with two, three rows of teeth. You can view anything through glass, but only your face. It is either inscribed as a kind of gullet or it is inside.

7: The listeners drifted back to the incubating hall. And outside, which was not visible. There was a reflection through panes of glass. Outside the brown Sqaumscott kept rising. It met challenges year by year. Plastics and runoff and all that. It worked above and below the falls, by then fully damned. Crickets in the land parcel signal solstice. Signal least amateur death. Cranes suspended their labor on the new gym.

8: When the reading ends, bodies exit without harm. Though, who knows what was contracted in that closeness. Meanwhile an actual body weighs up to 1,400 pounds. It moves under slow green currents. It swerves another boat, another summer. It is a purple smudge from a sea-plane. It is a movie-music muse. Each year the quarry moves further north. It can and cannot speak. Dropping teeth like petals along the fault. Picking up verbiage.

GIVEN STATES

The joke:
      always already looking
through the scope
what you saw was you
already
      looking.

*

*The installation was the last artwork D - - made. He left a stack
of Polaroids and a three-ring binder of detailed instructions for
assembly. What you see is a door, and in the door, two viewing
holes, and through the viewing holes, a body in repose in a
landscape backdrop. You cannot see a face, but a hand holds a
lamp. The canvas is behind the canvas, and behind it, layers of
shabby machinery. It is his life's work.*

*

Along the river
the thing you see and think you cannot have seen
makes you go on.

A woman seizes face-down in the reeds, black leggings pulled
down
to her ankles.

That nobody stops. That a moving body in the watery grass
is then not moving.

The speed of the parallel road.

*

When you look through the key, you see a woman.

Hers is the body who stands in for unnamed fear.

Like the black-suited stunt actor in her white crosses, she is
dubbed in.

A mirrored double.

She is an object of desire but also pitiful

as in a literal plane

for pity—otherwise

loss that only cannot be undone.

*

Yet the lamp suggests it can be undone

or is not done at all.

*

Seizing and still.

In repose
what we want to call a   *brutal aftermath*
a hand still holds a lamp
which must signify.

Or it is a joke.

A mirrored double.

In both landscapes, it is fall, and brown;
in both, the backdrops too blue for the occasion
and trees ornamental among the too-slow electric water like the
backdrop
of a a beer sign in a lonely bar—

*

D- - knew everything was a portrait.

Don't forget the workshop instructor said, he foremost had a great sense of humor.

All a body in a thing it made.

He knew that his body was the woman's body
and that he is both invoking
and rejecting sympathy.

To evoke and reject—
the function of the gesture
to conceal.

*We fill pre-existing forms and when we fill them we
change them and are changed.*

Looking through the scope you become the body splayed
and the leaves or lamps of us.

In the explosion of the plane,
the reality of the door is what is forgotten.

Bright spaces
and what is caught between them.

*

And then movement restored through the nasal passage: two pumps.

A movement in the reeds.

And the raising of the lamp.

CINEMA

Any two giant faces inclined to touch
in super 88 draw strings
over sawn spruce, evoke feelings—

love's event enlarged
so as to seem more true thereby
becomes truth—

//

What if singular feeling's negative plate
were blown up a thousand-fold
so any willing eye, spine-inclined could tilt

in shared half-dark and be forever
loved or loved
in an instant w/o post-script
which is eternal—blurred and gigantic, men
kissing in the black and white grammar
of the past and women
kissing?

//

You who share my air / dust
in (projections of xenon and mercury vapor-arcs)
and oxygenated water w/ corn syrup and sweet
oils, this feeling of desire alongside but not for
          or looking at Me,
could see me then as also alive
by mark of imitation—
R align this   { } :

After, we
walk w/o sound to our gorgeous cars
          in the fruit-bowl lot arced
in halogen to nurture from the same root
opposing fantasies—

TUMBLING WOMAN

Eric Fischl, 2002
Bronze sculpture

You don't want to see it.
Instinctual the way you reach
for a hand. The way anyone would.

Fall, we write, because *jump* implies
a choice that cannot be redeemed
or jump implies a choice and in a day

of unreal blue ("severe
clear") and in fire or heat and later, in rage, choice
is the verb that won't redeem.

In bronze the body does not "fall" but "tumbles"—
maybe or never makes contact with ground
that is always somewhere between zero

and an infinite number of seconds away.
She was displayed for about a week
then removed.

Outrage is a gulf between dust cells and story
and a clamp reiterates its power
by holding more sharply to what it suspends.

"The world prefers to remember images of
heroism" or to make them
because bodies in architecture are failures—

a problem: how to sort dust parts.
Another: images locked in images are ever-playable.
Always only momentarily forgotten.

In bronze her body does not "fall" but "tumbles";
this is a forever undoing. It maybe or never makes contact
with ground that is always between zero

and and infinite number of seconds away.
You don't want to see it. Hold out your hand—
the way anyone would—

WHEN YOU LOOK BACK AT THE YEARS THAT MADE YOUR OWN FACE

You see all loss is dust in water.
Everything solid stays and

      everything solid disappears.

In tragedy the one hero emerges
as anther left

      when its thin ruderals have blown all

away. What we don't say
is that the hero at the center

      decenters everything

else. No knowing of outside from
middle. See how easy what's true dissolves

      —in a film of sugar melting in oil

desire is made value by erasure.
How tender the breeze, rounded wings clear

      full as soap bubbles and as close

to the top—
how many bodies break for breathing

      now and after and in all time—

ankles glitter just above green surf
then under—follow me into

      the comedy of falling backwards.

The sky receding and cool
as I move back up, into shadows

                  of a neon-lit cave.

The hero is an engine
who darkens the screen—

                  is the finger drawing a thick line

of pain. Decades pass and oceans swell
beyond their fullness,

                  catch light

in just the right place.
An illuminated pane.

                  It hurts to catch—

I hope I can be caught.
On a stage, gorgeous

                  feathered eyes ask for life

falling so that others might see
the flames above.

                  We all fall

except those who, for now,
don't—safe for this moment, let

                  me hold you in my hands.

NOTES

I

"The Image 1: [Consumes the Event]" and "2: [Exalts the Event]" both draw their titles from Jean Baudrillard's essay *The Spirit of Terrorism*.

"Watching the Festival" is titled after the 2008 book of poems by Frank Bidart, *Watching the Spring Festival* (Farrar, Straus & Giroux). The lines, "you fashion your anger / to the world's anger" are an adaptation of two lines from Bidart's poem "The War of Vaslav Nijinsky" from *The Sacrifice* (Random House, 1983).

"Looking at You, Body" references John Singleton Copley's painting *Watson and the Shark* (1778) and James Abbott McNeill Whistler's painting *Nocturne in Black and Gold: The Falling Rocket* (1875). The lines, "you floated on the coffin / of the body of your friend" is a reference to the end of Herman Melville's *Moby Dick*.

"Light Sentence" is an ekphrasis of Mona Hatoum's installation art piece of the same name (1992).

II

"You Never Die the Evening [Before Your Death]" is an ekphrasis of artist Monika Bravo's film, "Uno Nunca Muere la Víspera." The film's title roughly translates to the poem's title. Monika Bravo had an art residency in the North Tower of the World Trade Center in September of 2001. On the evening of September 10, 2001, she recorded time-lapse footage of a storm passing over lower Manhattan. She collected the footage later that evening and did not return to her work space. She later compiled the footage into the above-titled film.

"[sound of water falling / and cars—]" is a concrete poem and also an ekphrasis of "Reflecting Absence," the sculpture designed by Michael Arad and Peter Walker to memorialize and mark the former location of the World Trade Center towers in lower Manhattan, New York. The shapes on the page approximate the shapes and spacing of the two memorial pools.

"Paper, Recovered" uses a handwritten note recovered on September 11, 2001, as its first few lines. I have kept most of the original annotations and added some of my own. The original note can be found at the 9/11 Memorial and Museum, or in their online archives.

"I Have Promises to Keep" is a near-abecedarian that lists, alphabetically, items recovered and archived on or after September 11, 2001, in New York. It is not a complete abecedarian, because there were no objects cataloged whose listed titles began with "X," "Y," or "Z." The title is from Robert Frost's "Stopping By Woods on a Snowy Evening," and the poem loosely adopts the structure and meter of Frost's poem.

"The Physical Impossibility Of" is a reference to and partial ekphrasis of Damien Hirst's installation piece, "The Physical Impossibility of Death in the Mind of Someone Living," which features a tiger shark preserved in formaldehyde.

"Given States"
This poem is an ekphrasis of an art installation of the same title ("*Étant donnés*") by Marcel Duchamp, held at the Philadelphia Museum of Art.

The line, "we fill pre-existing forms and when we fill them we change them and are changed" is from the poem "Borges and I" by Frank Bidart (*Desire*, Farrar, Straus & Giroux, 1999).

"Tumbling Woman" is an ekphrasis of a bronze sculpture by Eric Fischl that was created in part to memorialize the people who jumped or fell from the upper floors of the World Trade Center on September 11, 2001. Fischl created a series of these sculptures, some of which were exhibited to the public within a few years of the event. There was a public outcry in response to the sculptures' exhibition in New York, citing ongoing sensitivity. They were subsequently removed from viewing.

With Thanks

I am deeply grateful to the many people who have supported this project. Without you, none of my work would be possible. Special gratitude to Rory Brinkmann, Nikola Champlin, and Olivia Cook. I also offer thanks to my readers and supporters at conferences, including the team at Tupelo Press, my workshop group at the Bread Loaf Writers' Conference, and my monthly workshop group. I am additionally indebted to my great teachers and mentors, including Catherine Barnett and Heather Treseler, who kindly lent their words to this book's cover. Infinite gratitude, at last, to Anthony Walton, my mentor and former teacher from whom I learned what I needed to know most about writing poetry.

ABOUT THE COVER ARTIST

Todd Bartel's professional activities include artmaking, teaching, curating, research, and writing in Boston, MA, and the broader New England region. He received a BFA in painting from the Rhode Island School of Design and an MFA in painting from Carnegie Mellon University. He teaches drawing, painting, collage, and conceptual art at the Cambridge School of Weston (MA). Bartel's cover art is from his *Terra Reverentia* series, which explores the removal of humans and human activities from the definition of the word "nature." More of Bartel's work can be found at *toddbartel.com* or @collagehead on Instagram.

KB Kinkel is a poet, writer, and teacher based in New England. The recipient of the TQ32 Poetry Prize, he was longlisted for the Frontier Award for New Poets in 2023. KB's poems, essays, and book reviews have appeared or are forthcoming in *Tupelo Quarterly, Ninth Letter, Prelude, The Rumpus, Poetry Online,* and elsewhere. He holds an MFA in poetry from the University of Iowa Writers' Workshop and lives in Massachusetts, where he teaches high school English and creative writing. *Blood Machine*, the winner of the 2025 Finishing Line Press Chapbook Open, is his first book-length publication. More of KB's work and projects can be found at kbkinkel.com.

www.ingramcontent.com/pod-product-compliance
Lightning Source LLC
Chambersburg PA
CBHW020219090426
42734CB00008B/1140